Shadows

poems by

Kristin Bryant Rajan

Finishing Line Press
Georgetown, Kentucky

Shadows

Copyright © 2024 by Kristin Bryant Rajan
ISBN 979-8-88838-462-6 First Edition
All rights reserved under International and Pan-American Copyright Conventions. No part of this book may be reproduced in any manner whatsoever without written permission from the publisher, except in the case of brief quotations embodied in critical articles and reviews.

ACKNOWLEDGMENTS

"Eight Candles" comes from a creative nonfiction work "Eight Candles in September." *Watershed Review*; Pushcart and Best of the Net Nominee.
"My Grandmother's Funeral" in *Just A Little More Time: 56 Writers on Loss and Love*. Corbin Lewars, editor
"Sundays and Shadows." *Inscape Magazine*

Publisher: Leah Huete de Maines
Editor: Christen Kincaid
Cover and internal photos: © Laura Matthias Bendoly / Laura M. Bendoly Fine Art Photograph
Author Photo: Kristin Rajan
Cover Design: Elizabeth Maines McCleavy

Order online: www.finishinglinepress.com
also available on amazon.com

Author inquiries and mail orders:
Finishing Line Press
PO Box 1626
Georgetown, Kentucky 40324
USA

Contents

Eight Candles 1

Sundays and Shadows 9

Sunlit Silence 13

Birthday Parties and Funerals 21

"Compassion is born from understanding suffering."
Thich Nhat Hanh
To my father, with love and gratitude

Eight Candles

The house is still,
braced for the influx.

I prop myself against the wall
and wait,
hoping to absorb the cool, calm solidity from plaster.

A single swarm of children moves through the yard—
dancing, tumbling, singing,
with wild celebration in their eyes.

I listen to their laughter bouncing through the lawn—
high pitched chatter grows louder as they approach.

I am a loosened thread on the fringes of this tapestry;
though I'm supposed to be the center of the weave.

I see peripherally the swirling hues
of summer shorts and birthday hats.
But I am entranced by darkness beneath color,
a gloom behind neon orange and blue balloons
and shiny purple birthday plates.

I know now that there is shadow beneath pigment.

Silent with this secret,
I move through birthday motions.

My name is laced between plump, pasty roses
on the cake my mother bought
from the Farm Fresh down the street.
Bold, bright ribbons
on packages of all sizes and shapes
hold birthday promises in their glisten.

Every relative within miles
kneels down
close to me:
Their smiles carve crevices around their eyes;
their wide grins
uncover silver fillings and receding gums.

To look up at them takes too much strength,
so I look down,
to my Converse All Stars sneakers.
Hoping when I look up again,
they will be gone.

On this September day, I become an eight year old.

The setting sun releases crickets' songs,
and the sweet wet grass invites tug-of-war and dodgeball.

I try to play,
groping for movement
that will save me,
but I feel as if I'm sinking in the dew.
I can not divert my body
from the ball's oncoming orange
and am reminded of my weakness
when the impact takes my breath.

I know,
while aimless in this play,
that my mother stands in the kitchen's fluorescent glow,
contemplating the movement of her fingers
placing candles on the cake.

With even, ceremonial gestures,
she pushes rigid sticks of blue and pink and yellow wax,
just below the rainbow icing,
to the quick of the cake.

Is she thinking with each thin candle
what these eight years were to her?
Thrust into unplanned motherhood,
pushed deeper into wifehood,
these hoods hanging heavy over her,
blinding her from paths she might have taken,
hiding the beauty in her eyes,
hiding the beauty from her eyes.

Her silence sinks beneath
the candles' pastel colors
to the core,
the wick,
the truth
of what these eight years are for her.

The others don't yell at me for not playing;
they don't tell me to get out of the way.

Their movement is brisk and light,
propelled by childhood energy.
Their joyous screams
bob across the new-mown yard
like bird calls,
then amplify and rise above the oaks.
When one among them falls,
they laugh with their entire bodies.

But I stand still
awkwardly among them,
happy forms silhouetted,
children's faces shaded by a darker truth.

Do they see my stillness?
Do they hear the silence in my house?
Did they see the brown paper grocery bag
with my father's underwear and shaving cream?

Shortly before the candles are lit,
the bag is gone.

The rattle from his precarious muffler
is loud in the driveway,
fading as he drives down the street
and turns the corner out of view.

I still hear it when smiling faces sing.
I still hear it when I close my eyes to make a wish.

And after extinguishing each candle
with an exhausting breath,
a breath heavy with hope,
I still hear it.

Smoke pinches my eyes
when I open them to see
that nothing has changed,
that everything has changed
on this day that I turn eight.

As sticky squares of sweet are placed on plastic plates,
my dad finds a home in a motel room.
As my mother dishes Neapolitan ice cream
with soft, smooth hands,
he lights a joint
with calloused, bitten fingers,
watching the smoke seductively circle his head,
listening to paper burn as he sucks in,
breathing in the dance,
deep into his chest,
letting out what will not remain inside.

Pouring Hawaiian Punch and coffee,
my mother is as sweet
as the sugar-shortening frosted cake,
the perfect hostess.
She tucks away her sadness so deep behind her eyes,
she doesn't seem to see it.

She weaves among the relatives and children,
the strongest thread,
touching each stitch to hold this piece together,
to prevent my birthday from shredding at the seams.

The living room resonates with voices I know
and a choir of laughter.
But I only hear the clanging of my father's muffler
fading down the street.

I only see the empty places in our home.

The plastic fork feels heavy in my hands.
The small bite fills my mouth.
The sweetness coats my tongue and teeth.
I chew to stop my lips from twisting
to the contorted position of a cry.
I force my mouth into movement,
chewing harder to work loose the tightness of the jaw
just before the tears.

This September night,
I try to act with the grace and poise
of my seasoned mother.
I wear surprise and excitement
like a pinafore
as I strip the color from each gift.
I speak quickly,
with enthusiastic pitches,

but secretly censor every other word
so not to stumble on my sadness.

I wear the veil of my inheritance,
an heirloom of facades.

I am my mother's understudy.

But the latex of this mask
makes me hot and sweaty underneath.
And when the house is drained of people,
I am eager to emerge from my stifling disguise
and breathe in steady tempo.

In the quiet of the kitchen,
my mother washes remnants of the evening
from coffee cups.

I watch her back and neck
rise and fall with laden breath.

I lack the courage to confess my pain
for fear of reminding her of hers.

We roll into the waves of routine
and lose our footing.

On separate floors, we brush our teeth and wash our faces
while we listen to each other through metal pipes.

We never speak about the silence in our house.
We move quickly:
no time to talk;
no time to listen.

And after all is in its place—
the dishes, towels, and coffee cups—
we speed to sleep
and use illusions as our blankets
on that hot September night.

Sundays and Shadows

At our family cookout on the beach,
my father holds a joint,
squeezed tight between his thumb and forefinger.
It looks to me like a candy cigarette—
sweet sugar smoke
from a thin strip of white
that turns to bubblegum.

He squints his eyes,
breathes in the smog.
White paper burns and shrinks
with each deep inhalation.

With each weighted exhalation,
he drifts further away,
hidden behind gray smoke,
bereft of sweetness.

He meets a woman
where the waves break on the shore,
follows salt crystal prisms in her hair
deep into the sand dunes
where sedge grass hides them from sun
and eyes
and me.

When sand no longer holds the warmth of day,
my aunt and uncle take me home.

Even now, decades from that age of twelve,
charcoal and weed still smell the same.
The skunky smoke of both intermingle in my mind,
musky air to whet the appetite
for women who might pass by
and brittle burgers left too long on the grill.

I don't remember what we said
on Sundays,
our day together.

Through the smoke,
his face felt far away,
silent as stone.

Deadened by defeat:
a failed marriage,
a hated job,
a distant daughter.

Sometimes he smiled,
especially when a pretty girl was near,
but that was rare.
It was often just the two of us.
He had no reason to smile at me.

When there was a girlfriend in his life,
he'd make jokes and buy me ice cream cones.
We spoke a new name;
a new perfume
cloyed to the vinyl seats of his Datsun B210.

Then that one would disappear
and so would the ice cream,
and so would the laughter.

I tried to fill the silence
with the only small talk
one so small can find.

On Sundays,
my father lying on the couch
staring at an open window.

Leaning over him,
I strained to see
what it was he saw.

But I don't think he was looking at the trees
or the ornate shapes their shadows made on sidewalks.

I don't think he saw me
seeing him,
bending my body in ways that hurt
to try to find his view.

His vision clouded by his misery.

Sundays with Dad always ended with the sunset;
that's when he took me home.

I tried to make those Sundays feel like fun,
or even look like fun,
as if we could pretend they were fun.

I wanted to bring Sunday's light
inside my father's darkness.

But he was stuck inside the shadows
and I was too small to pull him out.

Sunlit Silence

My husband, two children, and I make the trip
from Atlanta, Georgia to Southeastern Virginia
as we do every year at Christmas,
when we pile into the car with dogs and gifts
and grumbles of
"Too many suitcases—
"What were you thinking?"
while loading and unloading the car.

But once settled in, irritation is glossed
by eggnog, mistletoe, pine,
and warm gatherings
at my grandmother's house.

But this time it's not Christmas:
it's mid-October.

This time we don't drive:
we fly—
because we need to get there fast,
because funerals don't wait,
because we didn't plan on this,
because it's all we can do.

We take turns
taking showers,
brush our hair,
wear skirts and suits—
just like we do each Christmas Eve.

But this time she will not greet us
with fragranced, soft skin,
sparkling costume jewelry,
and a hug that squeezes out
the sadness.

This is when we need that hug.

I never told her
how soft I found her skin,
how she smelled of lilacs,
how much I need her hugs.

My brother will carry the coffin.
He worries that his shoes are scuffed,
his thrift store suit too tattered.
In the last moments before leaving,
he dyes his shoes,
hoping they will dry quickly in the autumn sun.

But we all know
that she wouldn't mind scuffed shoes,
a tattered suit.

She only cared about the person.

In her last hours,
in a morphine sleep
my brother whispered in her ear,
"I love you."
He is sure her rhythmic snoring paused.
He is sure she heard him—
certainty softening pain.

Later that day,
my aunt held the phone to my grandmother's ear
so I could say from far away,
"You are everything to me."
Through tears and breaking voice,
I tried to be as clear, as strong, as she.

But her snoring never paused.
I don't think she heard me.

My father says repeatedly,
trying to convince himself,
"She wanted it this way."
And this is true.

Every time I saw her,
for years,
maybe for decades,
she'd say,
"Don't you be sad for me when I'm gone.
I want you to know that I'm ready any time."

She was at peace with an imminent end
for years.

But I never was,
which she knew,
which is why she kept reminding me,
which is why my father keeps reminding us
that she wasn't sad about dying.

So why are we so sad?

My mother,
my grandmother's ex daughter in-law,
prefixes and suffixes
offering good excuse for distance,
was my grandmother's closest friend—
indicative of how love abides
when people are loving.

My grandmother answered all my mother's questions
about teething, sleeping, potty training.

Advice given
only when asked,
never unsolicited,

because unsolicited advice is hostility,
because my grandmother had no hostility.

My aunt, my age,
in my grandmother's words
her "saving grace"
for a 45 year old woman who needs to nurture
when her adult children have left home,
speaks of the address book—
pages soft with age,
decades of dwellings,
scratched out when people moved,
replaced with a new house number,
street and zip code,
kept up to date until the end—
though the handwriting becomes less precise.

Who will be the hub now?
Who will keep front doors wide open
for anyone who's passing through?
Who will take the time to sit and talk
anywhere,
at any time,
knowing that conversation is all that matters,
that dust and dishes wait,
that heartfelt words are life.

The only time she ended a conversation
was when another one began—
and now.

My grandmother recorded her funeral on a cassette tape
years before she died—
her story, her life, in her voice,
with music laced between the words.

She played her funeral for us with pride in her eyes.

We sat around the kitchen table
listening to her art,
the story of her life.

We told her it was beautiful,
but we didn't want to think of it,
didn't want to envision her not with us.

But with all she created
in her very creative life,
her funeral for herself
was her most inspired piece:
her life,
her words,
with music that meant the most.

This was her masterpiece.

Sitting in the church
that mid-October afternoon
we hear that work again.

The sun illuminates her face
still within the coffin.
Her voice fills the sanctuary with softness,
a kind-hearted southern grace,
making it feel that she is with us.

I listen to her voice
while looking at her face,
so close to how it used to be,
but so, so very different.

I'm hungry for her words
in her own voice,
cling to every detail:
her life as young Glenelle,

in the North Carolina tobacco fields,
mesmerized by the moon;
her infatuation with my grandfather,
the dashing sailor who came into the diner where she worked,
ate her fried chicken and collard greens,
said they were the best he'd ever had;
the deep, enduring love for her four children,
her seven grandchildren,
and her six great-grandchildren.

She earned her titles Grand and Great.

An oral story
full of love, friendship, laughter, pain,
and music.

She speaks of peace with death,
as she always did in life.

Then in the church
with her so close,
her story ends.

Her voice is gone—
abrupt, complete
silence.

No words, no music:
no Glenelle
no
grandmother, mother, wife, aunt, friend, confidante.

No comfort.

Just silence.

Her stillness in the coffin
and empty
hollow
aching
sunlit
silence.

Birthday Parties and Funerals

After my grandmother's funeral,
I prepare for the next big event:
my 50th "surprise" party.

The date set long ago,
an empty room reserved,
food ordered.

The show must go on.
I prepare my face for the look of fun.

My husband has been planning this party
since he forgot my 40th birthday a decade ago.
He asked permission because I hate surprises.
My consent was more a gift to him.

Days of decorations, invitations, gathering photos of me in my youth.

I waiver between gratitude that he would do this for me
and dread of impending attention,
my aging projected in photos on a screen,
the fear that someone will see the sadness in my eyes—
then and now.

The friend who drives me
pulls into a parking lot I've never seen.

I see my father leaning against his car,
smoking a joint,
reminding me how long I've felt this pain
on this, my 50th birthday.

So many birthdays, holidays, Sundays
marked by the pungent smoke
that muted all the colors.

A somber note to begin the night,
before entering a dark, quiet room,
which erupts into fluorescence and loud coached joy:
"SURPRISE!"

A room full of friends and smiles and me—
a jolting reminder of the passage of time
by those who love me most.

The night unfolds under an autumn moon—
wine, beer, music, chicken bites, and sweet potato chips,
more wine and beer.

The height of heels piled against the wall
measures the pleasure on the dance floor.

The moon moves across the sky;
friends find their shoes and stumble home.

I survive birthday attention;
the celebration passes.

In bed, I close my eyes
bid fond farewell to forced fun and social perspiration.

I hear my father in the next door bathroom,
heaving, coughing, gasping,
the violent sounds of human expulsion—
purging the toxicity of too much.

Through deep gutteral groans,
he disembowels himself
of his own poison.

He collapses
on bathroom tile,
falling into sharp shooting pain,
a samurai falling on his sword

barely whispering
 "intolerable"
"excruciating"—
exhausted by mere syllables.

I peel clothes from his humid body,
the threadbare dress pants he's worn
for years of special occasions,
the ones he wore to his mother's funeral last week.

His flaccid, small bottom hangs from his hips.

He is smaller than I remember—
a little boy whose mom has left him.

I am now the 50 year old daughter who washes him.

I move him from bed to bath to bed.
No place or posture offers comfort.

I take him to the hospital,
where doctors dance
then trip around the terms
"alcoholism"
"pancreatitis"
"cannabinoid hyperemesis."
Words as familiar to me as
Sunday or birthday.

"Sleep" my father pleads,
"please, just make me sleep."

And so they do:
pump him full
of liquids, medicines—
anti-nausea, sleep inducers,
numbing fluids.

Some drugs add what's good;
others take away what's bad,
the way the weed and alcohol were supposed to work.

As he sleeps,
his face softens,
finally transported to a simple place,
of childhood sun that doesn't sear the skin,
of baseball fields filled with laughter,
when his mother softly stroked his hair,
when fun wasn't artificially induced,
when the passage of time was nothing to escape,
when there was nothing to fear,
when funerals were rare
if ever.

A place
where birthdays were always happy,
sparkling with effervescent laughter,
paper pointed hats, frosted cakes,
and joyful, lilting songs.

"Happy Birthday to you.
Happy Birthday to you.
Happy Birthday DEAR…"

A place where he felt
dear,
loved,
cherished.

Kristin Bryant Rajan, PhD in English, writes poetry, fiction, creative nonfiction, and literary criticism in Atlanta, GA and is a senior lecturer in English at Kennesaw State University. She is widely published in creative writing journals and anthologies as well as literary and academic journals and books. Her writing, academic and creative, and her teaching revolve around the power of perspective. She firmly believes that writing and literature are paths to peace, power, and well-being.

Her creative work affirms that compassion and healing stem from understanding and writing is a way to understand. She is a Pushcart and Best of the Net nominee. Her creative work can be found in *The Watershed Review, Apeiron Review, Parks and Points, Fredericksburg Literary and Art Review, Postcard Poems and Prose Magazine, Inlandia: A Literary Journal*, among others, and the anthologies *Moon Days, Just a Little More Time, Rorschach's Ink,* and *Surprised by Joy*, among others.

Her criticism investigates Buddhism and meditative moments of deep self in modernist literature, particularly the works of Virginia Woolf. She has written on the role of nature, fashion, racism, and social media as they apply to identity and literature. She has a chapter in the forthcoming *The Edinburgh Companion to Virginia Woolf and Transnational Perspectives*, Edinburgh University Press, on attire, selfhood, Woolf, and Gucci and is currently writing a book on Buddhist moments of deep self in the works of Virginia Woolf. Her criticism highlights the role of performance and external representations of self as well as the recognition of a deeper, flowing selfhood beneath the surface, illuminating peace and interconnection. In addition to Virginia Woolf, she has written on William Wordsworth, Katherine Mansfield, James Joyce, Anne Patchett, and Joyce Carol Oates.

As a senior lecturer at Kennesaw State University, she teaches English from the perspective that writing and literature can not only enrich but can also save our lives. Many students entangled in webs of social media pressures, political divides, and climate change concerns find empowerment through writing and literature, commenting that her classes are transformative.

She facilitates happiness and meditation workshops that integrate her research on mindfulness and well-being. And she also teaches lively Spin classes at the Decatur YMCA, playing carefully curated music loudly and mixing cardio and humor, with the firm believe that laughing is the most healing exercise of all.

All her interests are coalescing in exciting ways, and she finds her writing, research, teaching, and life are extensions of her daily meditation practice, leading her to the gifts in the present (get it?).

You can find her at kristinrajan.com; Instagram and Facebook @ *kristin.bryant.rajan.*

www.ingramcontent.com/pod-product-compliance
Lightning Source LLC
Chambersburg PA
CBHW040308170426
43194CB00022B/2946